# SKIN, INC.

BOOKS BY THOMAS SAYERS ELLIS

Skin, Inc.

The Maverick Room

Song On (chaplet)

The Genuine Negro Hero (chapbook)

# SKIN, INC.

Identity Repair Poems by

# THOMAS SAYERS ELLIS

GRAYWOLF PRESS

This publication is made possible by funding provided in part by a grant from the Minnesota State Arts Board, through an appropriation by the Minnesota State Legislature, a grant from the National Endowment for the Arts, and private funders. Significant support has also been provided by Target; the McKnight Foundation; and other generous contributions from foundations, corporations, and individuals. To these organizations and individuals we offer our heartfelt thanks.

NATIONAL ENDOWMENT FOR THE ARTS    MINNESOTA STATE ARTS BOARD    WELLS FARGO    TARGET.

Special funding for the publication of this volume has been provided by the Jerome Foundation.

Published by Graywolf Press
250 Third Avenue North, Suite 600
Minneapolis, Minnesota 55401

www.graywolfpress.org

Published in the United States of America

ISBN 978-1-55597-567-8

2 4 6 8 9 7 5 3 1
First Graywolf Printing, 2010

Library of Congress Control Number: 2010922920

Cover design: Kyle G. Hunter

Cover photo: Portrait of Chinyere Evelyn Uku by Thomas Sayers Ellis, 2009

FOR YOU

# CONTENTS

SKIN, INC.

## As Segregation, As Us

Everything supposedly "like" something else, or forced into skin,
has already been taken advantage of
by an Aesthetic (Affirmative) Action.
If we could measure the integrity of a simile,
it wouldn't be any different.
        Those who know this also know
some content of struggle,
their lives and lines built less to break
than to last,    never thinking shit
like    Should the body govern the next line
        or the mind?

Shut up about Sameness. Shut up about Difference.

I don't allude like you. I don't call me anything.

These genres these borders these false distinctions
are where we stay at
in freedom's way.

*Or,*


Or Oreo, or
worse. Or ordinary.
Or your choice
of category

      or
      Color

or any color
other than Colored
or Colored Only.
Or "Of Color"

      or
      Other

or theory or discourse
or oral territory.
Oregon or Georgia
or Florida Zora

or
Opportunity

or born poor
or Corporate. Or Moor.
Or a Noir Orpheus
or Senghor

or
Diaspora

or a horrendous
and tore-up journey.
Or performance. Or allegory's armor
of ignorant comfort

or
Worship

or reform or a sore chorus.
Or Electoral Corruption
or important ports
of Yoruba or worry

or
Neighbor

or fear of . . .
of terror or border.
Or all organized
minorities.

## My Meter Is Percussive

so throughout this worry,
I am rolling my eyes.

I am sucker-punching I,
the I that informs

these lines    like
only I    know I    know how.

I am breathing,
repairing, breathing,

half-interested in progress
and half-interested

in progression, never finished.
I am not a unit

of geography or grace.
My vocal skin

fragments, but not
like a secretary to eloquence.

If negritude, it fits
better than any

metaphor for river,
weary mask, or light-skinned religion.

I no longer write
white writing

yet white writing
won't stop writing me.

In life, they clutch
their purses because

they     want you     to think
you've stolen     something.

In art, they clutch
their purses because

they know     you know
they've stolen     something.

Most times, *yo*, the flow
of my own

Blackness
freedoms to defend me.

This lyric body,
a prosody, sentenced.

## Spike Lee at Harvard

[Five Joints]

At the Grolier, I was
 the shipping clerk,
employed in a corner
slim enough for a book.
I was surrounded by books,
by boxes of books,
and photographs of poets
and by customers
who loved poetry
and by famous poets
who were also customers
and that is where
I got my first glimpse
of the life of poetry
(through the Grolier's
cinematic glass window)
and where the life of poetry
first governed me,

toward discipline and surrender,
to work through
a mandate of silence,
so as not to "take advantage"
of my "position,"
as if any black person
would want to use
shipping and sweeping
to create an audience
for apprenticeship.

The Grolier's interior
was all literary integrity
and repetition, as if lit
by the alliterative gaze
of illiterate, lettered spirits,
its own elite enemy
of non-intellectuals
and integration. "Should we
separate the black poets
from the white poets
to make it easier
for customers to find
African American work,"
my employer asked.
Well, at least she asked.
One part of me thought,
"What's wrong with
this white woman?"
And the other part
. . . thought, "Hell No!"
but all I said was,
"I  don't  think  so,"
. . . said it slowly, so
as to suggest
the lyric range of attitude.
Another, mo betta, way
to frame this is to say that,
then, there was only
one black poet
on the wall of photographs,
Ai, interrupting

the white typeface
of American detachment.
A single profile of personas
like a caesura
in buttermilk.

A sonnet surrounded
by the shadows of ideas
and knives of artificial light,
the Grolier was
day for night
for nothing
but their work
and their likeness,
the colorless absence
of noise between
images and words.
Shelving was like casting;
being up on the ladder
like directing, all perspectives
of craft mine to theft.
*Yes!* Letterpress chapbooks,
signed overstock,
folded broadsides. *No!*
Of all the books I'd stolen,
I'd never stolen from the Grolier,
but you would not
have known that
from the auctioneer's way
she moved through my work,
like an apparition of inventory
chained to suspicion.
Three times around
the center display table,
under which Pumpkin
the shop's dog slept,
was like one time around

Ben Hur's Coliseum, in
Hulot's hiccupping jalopy,
as publishing, like
the Gulf War, filled
the world with
more ghosts.

In my other life,
 I was given an audience,
the keys to darkness,
an office of shadows,
and an editor's sense
of control over
my own crew of light.
Forgive me, champions
of Identity Politics,
for not just saying:
I had an evening job
as a projectionist-security guard
at the Harvard Film Archive,
in the last line
of Le Corbusier's
ramped prose poem
of glass and stone,
whose screen, like big paper,
was wide as the sky
and less restricted
than the Grolier's
marquee-like anthology
where the white people
in the framed photographs
rejected the glamour
of the white people
in movie stills.
My favorite being the photograph
of Gordon Cairnie,
the shop's original owner,
and Louisa Solano,

his young assistant,
locked in their
own couplet
for final cut.

As auteur, as author,
 I pray this last stanza
won't fade or break
into whiteness, the tense silence
at the end of rioting.
Down there, in the sync
between thinking and feeling,
this is where the soundtrack
would begin if poetry
paid enough for one
and if the public paid
more for poetry.
Dear Listener, are you
as swollen by this as I was living it,
these five different takes
of the same sickness?
Already, you must
be tired of these uneven
four, five and six word lines.
If so, toss a trash can,
like a lidless metaphor,
through this poem's
narrative, wild style
into the sepia flashback
of any number of book parties.
For every insult
and broken promise,
the crash, a critical review,
the flying glass.
Poets running
for cover with nothing

to cover themselves
but their own book covers.
Call the cops if you like.
Their slanted shadows
can't spell a hold
on craft.

All growth is a result of freedom. A culture grows or is restricted depending largely on how hospitable it is to ideas from outside, or how freely it delves into itself, renovating traditional insights into a contemporary diction. A culture is also a state of constant and often unrelated activity: *dynamism* and *culture* are two words often paired together, and are a measure of the health and growth of a culture. Another way of looking at culture is to see how susceptible it is to prejudice, in any form—how resistant it is to uncritical acceptance of "accepted ideas," or, on the other hand, how easily it succumbs to any idea which is negatively propounded, i.e. one that is accompanied by fanaticism or dogmatism in its believers. A very good measure of a culture is indeed in its ability to take apart or neutralize a negative dogmatism.

Rajat Neogy

I

## The Return of *Colored Only*

One of these badass,
glorious days,
the signs and negative sounds
that worked against us

will all begin their tenures
of service, their holy and complex repentance.
It has already begun with
"Nigger" and "Bitch"
and for this we have young folks to thank,
their disrespect and fearlessness.

Naturally, this will scare
the civil rights out of some
and, for a mad-moment, empower
a great many wrong-cultured others.

To this "The Return . . ."
will either code switch or hood ornament,
drama-drumming both—a cult-nats matrimony
of the vernacular remix: ain't studin' you,
nommo no more nommo,
stop studin' us.

All yall who tell yall hearts *Art*,
your Bama Hour is, again, up-struggling
as we (credits and debits alike)
hang and unhang the old slanders ourselves

—not as segregationists
(although that wouldn't be
that bad, given . . .) and not as Air Februarians
(. . . , given . . .) but as identity repair-people,
faders of trick moves, trope-a-dopes
and okee dokes,

laying our dice down like (      ) like we love us.

# II

# Song On

The next word has the sound of the last and the next.

Taban Lo Liyong

Our little columns of expletives,
of noise so uppity
it looks down on nuance
even as it battles poverty
and the battles with poverty

we disguise
as battles with each other.

Our own ideas of mastery,
of property of, of ourselves,
our highest and lowest selves,
is literacy, is us, we wearing nothing (to prove) ness,
in service of, of survival,

of structural integrity,
the idiom-drum of control.

We don't but they do    they understand
we are weapons
and if we weapon we win.
Thus this must flood    many others
and other    many flooders

if only to prevent syntax,
the torturer's deep linguistic cover,

from crippling
the victim's workforce of tongues,
and the page
from behaving like bad public assistance.
Flat, fixed and finished.

# III

## Understanding the New Genuine Negro Hero

For
never
gets a thing, ever.
Our range of high-worries, the low-joys,
every, flava-sealed

fracture, the folk
and uppity nuances of "being bla . . ."
not "happens to be . . . ,"

from the triflin'
to the bougie, the coon to the revolutionary,
the bama to the buppie.

A ghetto celeb might *kick it*
with a hood rat,
but a *for real for real* sistuhgirl

ain't likely to be seriously
*stepped to*
by Big Willie or a baller.

Without the Mountainbottom,
the Mountaintop
is just another government name.

I didn't Overcome.
This the same me I was before
skin's melanin whip,

coloring color the color
I want to color color, not the color
color colors me.

Mighty Whitey loves the cold,
so soon as I see a noose
somebody gettin' they aesthetic whooped.

Go'ne make that disrespectful paper.
More melon than water
is good
for you,
seeds too.

## The Identity Repairman

### AFRICAN

I am rooted.
Ask the land.
I am lyric.
Ask the sea.

### SLAVE

America is where
I became an animal.
America is where
I became a nigger.

## NEGRO

Trapped here
in Segregation.
Trapped here
in Integration.


## COLORED

I am weary of working
to prove myself equal.
I will use education
to make my children superior.


## BLACK

My heart is a fist.
I fix Blackness.
My fist is a heart.
I beat Whiteness.


## AFRICAN AMERICAN

Before I was born,
I absorbed struggle.
Just looking
at history hurts.

## Ways to Be Black in a Poem

You'll need a talk, an oral walk,
Something natural and recognizable by your folk,
Something of music something of meaning,
A style capable of running-off-at-the-mouth
When Massa AmEuroBrit Lit irks you most,
A little something-something of ancestry
And the courage not to accept any award

      that helps you
      and hurts others.

You'll need "Saturation,"
Your own profanity of Sundays,
Breakfast and Black fist.
Wherever there is living You must listen
For the    *if* and *when*    the vernacular gives birth, again.
You will need more than reference
Coulda    woulda    shoulda
And more than edjumacation.

You may even need to sell you and buy you,
     So low
         So long
             Sold
Or to slant yourself into a container whose symbolism
Is unknowingly superior
To standard usage,

A brilliant attitude loved by good.

## AWS Ode

[African Writers Series]

So long a letter,
the slums numbered spines
and night fell
bright as the will to die, or the joys of motherhood.
Its beautiful feathers.

Black and white in love.
The wound is proof
"of how terrible orange is," black sunlight.
Here is Nuruddin's *Sardines,*
but beware soul brother

the thirteenth sun
is a child of two worlds.
A hammer blows its ambiguous adventure.
Because of women,
a woman in her prime,

Zambia shall be free.
The smoke that thunders, thunders like a sunset in Biafra.
Robben Island regret
 is worse than
Lokotown neglect.

 Girls at war with a question of power
like Efuru and Idu
survive the peace like wrong ones on the dock.
 The mangy-dog we killed
detained interpreters.

 A blade among the boys,
bound to violence, ripples in the pool.
Maybe the mourned one
 was a naked needle riding on the whirlwind.
A man of the people.

 Maru, bewitched, Maru,
going down river road, eating chiefs, their dead roots,
will kill you quick,
 quicker than this earth, my brother.
The barbed wire satellites.

 A simple lust, the smell of it,
ordained by the oracle.
Remember Rubens' masterful use of silhouette.
 Small pass books with
powerful faces, passports.

Wirriyamu, an ill-fated people,
the grass is singing
not even God is ripe enough.
 Devil on the cross, my Mercedes is bigger than yours,
your narrow path's uneven ribs.

 Some short century for sure,
the busiest political spider web in nature
and this most difficult thing
 to hold together, was held together by Heinemann,
the healer of
God's bits of wood.

*Mr. Dynamite Splits*

[James Joseph Brown, Jr.]

Long before the patriot acts
of anthems "Say It Loud, I'm Black and I'm Proud,"
"Funky President" and "Living in America,"
you and your Revue were

the only flames the hood could afford,
and by "hood" I mean "nation"
and by "nation" I mean "community"
and by "community"

Already standing on the page, now it's time to consider the anatomy of the microphone.
How to handle it, as Mr. or Mrs.? Hear the dramatic swirl of strings like at the beginning
of "It's a Man's Man's Man's World" then hold the first note as long as you like before
jerking the reading-body into the percussive-lipped Intro and mouth-roofed tongue riff
of "ou," "our" and "ue." Across the white seats of silence between the stage-like stanzas,
emphasizing the I's until they are equal.

I mean any one of the various
Black "folk" Americas
within Black America,
the Constitution's future re-framers.

Your famous flames
were not the famous flames
of Civil War or Civil Rights.
These flames were raw chicken guts

An all within one, the soul of many, every read note. Emphasize "folk" as poly-purpose, the hardest working utterance—k to c and c from lower to upper case, the protest of climb and crash into law. Stage, stanza, some silence, a moment of preface, of breathing, before the door of pronoun. One must recite the emergence of fire so that it becomes attitude, weather and aesthetic.

and a bewildered next-time fire
of choked chords and percussive horns
Papa lit the behinds
of new bags with.

To quote Sweet Charles, *Yes it's you*
the warm globe mourns . . .
for passing mashed potatoes and peas.
Gimme some more.

Call to mind the "be" from "be f-o-r-e" from the preface to the poem and make the "be" in "bewildered" an echo and extension. Do this in the mind near the remembrance of Papa, southern-styling your young "be"hind. Your voice, when reading, must not rest in any one bag. Passing is not rest. Like you, the gesture and line must "unit of gimme" some "unit of more." A poem is just some.

No. 1, not because of the hits
but because the roads,
like Augusta, lead all back to you.
Georgia might not-never let us bury you.

The hellish crossroads of black genius
(not geography) left you leathery as Miles.
Not the first to smack-your-bitch-up
and stick-it-to-the-man,

Constructed on "No," on almost a stutter, the punch (as resistance to waiting for change) must arrive at both ends of the line. Both being ones, "on the," the guttural groan that becomes Georgia. If such ground can make genius a verb, then the dark geography of the JB 'phabet is a room we should go more often. Don't be so academic, so straight, you scared to smack and stick and bitch and it. Bottom of shoe should slide, head snap forward, forward and back, referencing 'petition.

but the first to smack-your-bitch-up,
stick-it-to-the-man,
fine your band, tour Vietnam,
serve two drummers,

fire your band, tour Africa,
save the Boston Garden, endorse Nixon,
rehire your band, sue a Rap group
and start a choir in prison.

Hear, here, the vowels of rigid leadership lift like a leg while the other one pretends to buckle in elastic structural support. The flutter of bones accepting horns. Know thyself, reader, well enough to honor "fine," "fire" and "rehire" without privileging either. Squeeze in a "jump-back," then in the stanza break, kiss thy self bad and soul bow.

Pre Hip Hop, you had your own emcee,
your own dancers, your own cape,
Lear jet and crown.
You graduated Super Bad.

Dr. King called it Drum Major Instinct.
Shirley Chisholm,
unbought and unbossed.
Damn right you were somebody.

Three p's so they get the feelin' and ride the long e even as you repeat the idea of ownership. Subtext Capitalism (Black), so don't get mad if someone throws a dollar on stage while you are reading. Land on "Bad" then use the sound-imagist known as esophagus to holla at your own orchestra of kidney, lungs, and liver. To complete the howlin' werewolf kit, show up in a perm and moustache.

"These nuts," that's what all the Camel Walks,
splits, spins and Popcorns
told those early closed doors.
Get up offa that thang.

Long live your plea please pleases,
Byrd's brotherly loyalty,
and calling-on Maceo's licking-stick.
*Live at the Apollo* laid legend to myth.

Grown ass male physical solo with real references to animal behavior, and the freedom-hesitation to lean back, scream and jump. Fists up to the face, body tightening—a prep for flow, like a brother getting some no matter who is looking. Sweet life I do. Get the "long" and the "loyalty" and the "licking" and the "live" and the "laid" and the "legend" all on the same time and they'll remember your shine. Eyes will catch the hits before they syllable the ground.

Before Hammer Time,
there was a time when "whatsinever" you did,
you did "to death."
Funky Broadway.

Your *eeeeeeeeeeeyow* will never rest.
You remain proud, cold bodyheat and sweat,
that muthafucka Black Caesar,
the only one who ever murdered dying.

This is the stanza to knock 'em dead but the page does not allow for a poetic equivalent of showstopper. These words are surrounded by silence, white space and white space is not an audience, not a living one, and neither is time. Every dance you know is an anti-grammar of another dance you do not know. All aboard with horns at your elbows, your chicken-scratched knees. Each a scarred vowel, night-training out from the steering sternum, on time.

Wasn't Jesus born today?
The Big Payback: the Angel Pneumonia
(not escape-ism) calling
the Godfather only halfway home.
What you gon' play now?

Stand, unfinished, like you are buried there until someone unburies an *Amen*. The room is just a room. You are the published radio, tuned, one of the ones dialed.

*Audience*

Imagine a door, a door
with a sign on it, a sign that excludes you.
Not a symbol of you,
but the real birth you: erased, gone.

Through the door,
something you think you want,
something you were told was in books,
a false wholeness: Europe.

And if you are lucky . . . a seat on one
of its not so murderous seas,
surrounded by listeners
who are "kind of" open.

So you go, alone in the mind, often,
despite the sign on the door
and the signs inside,
and you never come back.

You are rewarded for this, in public,
and accepted onto
their realm of podiums.
Disliked, by a few, too.

## The Obama Hour

*Finally*, one of us is properly
positioned to run. By "us" I mean Black,
by "positioned" I mean White
and by "run" I mean Race and its varied speeds of darkness,
the way "silver writes" faster than revolution
and the lit and darkening skin of the sky.
The triumphant exasperation, though, belongs
to the word "finally" with its slanted *f*
signifying relief, a "'bout time" up from the reservoir
of coded sighs we make to mask time,
Colored People's Time, our well-known resistance
to the Romanized face of the clock. To discuss running,
running the country, a black man running,
an African running America, you must discuss Race
including the difficult qualifying times
between the theft of our arrival and all hate crimes.
Race as gift, as campaign donation, and gifts matter.
It's racist to erase Race (because "erase"
means Blackness, ethnic cleansing,

get rid of the Blacks); and worse to hack off history
or any limb at any time, except for purposes
of assimilation and modern design.
In place of the usual halo of numbers, orange balls and spindles.
Lazy, often late for work, our walk a discourse,
shifting, like the unemployed shadow of a brother leaning on a corner.
But America prefers Religion to Race
and a clock has disciples, hours,
cuckoos and cock-a-doodle dos.
The people "go to sleep" and the people "wake up" to nature,
nations and denominations of,
not the bedside duet of alarm and digital glow.

## No Easy Task

Suddenly our names
were more than our own,
our dramas too. And,
as if the craft of our
inherited calling had only
two camps of Blackness,
"Academic" and "Spoken Word,"
our best work, the work
for all work, had to work
on the page (if we wanted
to be published) and
on the stage (if we wanted
to be recorded) . . . but, mostly,
we just wanted to be whole
(respected and known) and
heard (reviewed and enjoyed)
as in, in the tradition of "worriation"
and ". . . a loud noise followed
by many louder ones."

And not always as lonely as an "I"
and not always as burdened as a "we"
and never anyone's token,
hyphen, bridge, honorary anything,
or literary pet . . . even if
the listeners weren't reading
what we were scribbling
and the readers weren't listening
to what we were spitting . . . even if
an Open Mic never opened
an open book, *haters,*
and an opened book
never booked an Open Mic,
*favorites.* An ironic browbeat
if you a sonnet. If you a star
you wish you were higher,
a sermon. Enter audience,
the audio antithesis
of academia, worrying
text to talk and talk to text.
How . . . entertainment, poor folk-prosody,
oral jewelry, flow? The problem
with American poetry
is there's not enough Africa
in it; bling-bling has more
rhythm and imagery
than all of Ashbery.
At the edge of Subject,
poetics. At the center
of Subject, prose.
The uneven ribs of verse,

with its progression
of resurrections, reverses.
Outdated show-offs
like villanelles and sestinas,
pretending not to perform,
costume form. The content
of character, not the shape
of content, shapes form.
There's no such thing
as formlessness. *Applause.*
All poems perform.

*Skin, Inc.*


A black arm, unarmed, bent upward
at the elbow
so the blow slides off.
Wanted so bad,
        back then, to hit back
but didn't dare, ever, strike their tense, twisted spin.
Their ruled, loose-leaf,
paged air.
First they conjugate you,
then you die.
Them, laying out by their lonesome, blocking sun.
        You, shirtless, serving drinks,
one of the brown things they bleach, eat.
If punctuation
were a punch,
I'd publish line breaks of fists.
Sorry    I know
"Cracker" and "Honky" hurt,
but nothing fruits a noose like the N-word,

white acceptance or revolt.
No more little boxes,
stacked, like the ones in poems.
A deeper sense of verse frees skin.
I am not merely *in*

        this thing I am *in*. I am *it*.
Born in the morning to reform form's broken economy.
To sit-in
in the sit-in
in the margins.

*Smudge*


A

In nature, always reality. In art, always nature.
        If representational,
the recognizable governs technique.
If freer than figurative,
        you can feel the object
referencing a primitive system of punishment.
Beneath the skin, *brushstroke brushstroke*, bruise.
To express Expressionism, the thumb of time
smears humanity, blurring history.
Truth, too, contributes to the pain-pulse of memory
as if color, complexion and flesh-spectrum,
as if, and only if, the materials
are men, women and children.
All in their greasy mornings.

B

A good exhibition decomposes theory
but the dead in the work remain dead, swirling reminders
        of evil's palette,
pre-blister and post-burn.
The only thing surreal about weeping
are all the eyes, the catalogued ones lost to erasure.
The real map of mercy is here,
animated in Oil on Cotton
like the path water makes through abstract stone.
Shadow, Ashcan, shadow.
Victims lined up, awash in the violence of vision.
Ghost-portraiture, shroud.

C

This is what "resilience" looks like
from a sensitive satellite.
I almost wrote "suffering" but I chose "resilience" instead,
thinking of how wet paint can help the body
        accept opening earth.
Some sense of all of the elements is here.
Depth of fear, harrowing despair.
Some sense the torturer, lost in layering, an aerial gaze.
Not being able to make out a face or a family
does not diminish these deformed, sacred forms.
Anonymous artifice or known remembrance,
some smudges haunt the soul
        with hurt
bright as a cemetery of yellow, human flora.

D

Many of the images melt
while others appear to rumor, ghetto-fashion,
into one another.
        White is not used to heaven, only to accent
un-witnessed regions of grief.
I like it when range finder, breathing plastic
        and messy rainbows collide.
Even the self, as graphite,
seems less dimensional than handwriting.
Gravediggers, too, owe something to perspective.
Art can rip the skin off of a cherry picker
the same way the sky above an Opening
        can become a solid.
Private collections are worse; they hide proof.

# TWO MANIFESTOS

## The New Perform–A–Form

[A Page Versus Stage Alliance]

The performance body, via breathing and gesture, dramatizes form. It makes it theater. It makes it action. It makes it living, alive, as in "get live," as in "all the way live," as in lyric. The idea body, via text and thought, flattens form. It makes it fixed. It makes it language. It makes it literature, an imagined living, as in artifice. The work of the performance body is not without craft, control or form. It is not lowly. The work of the idea body is not without attitude, improvisation or flow. It is not closed. A perform–a–form occurs when the idea body and the performance body, frustrated by their own segregated aesthetic boundaries, seek to crossroads with one another. This coupling, though detrimental to aspects of their individual traditions, will repair and continue the living word.

# One

The old style of representing "likeness" is over and perform–a–formers, though appreciative of metaphor and simile, no longer need either to express nuance in poetry. The matrimony of page and stage insists on eliminating the false functions between the line and the limb. All rhyme schemes reborn as gesture, all gestures as sculptural integrity.

# Two

A perform–a–form line breaks many times, verbally, before it breaks the last time visually. If written, it is written more like blood than bone. If spoken, it is spoken more like stutter than song. Perform-a-forms do not lie (on the page or on the stage), frozen in little boxes or voices, unable to interact with the reader or listener, as if on a table in a morgue.

# Three

Perform–a–formists seek a path around both Academic and Slam Poetry, to eliminate the misconceptions between them, and to balance the professional opportunities (in publishing and employment) opened to each. The utterance, paged or memorized, is only a schema in need of diverse modes of respiration.

## Four

Against the narrowness of linearity, a perform–a–former will subject its own composer-sition to the rigor of audience participation. You can't workshop a perform–a–form but you can participate in its creation and correction. Able to surrender to the collective sensibility of community, not the critic's scalpel, the last great perform–a–former was Sekou Sundiata.

## Five

A well crafted perform–a–form will continue to pour after it is written or performed. This pouring, akin to echoing, should reclaim the original attributes of poetry from nature and cinema. Despite history, the perform–a–poet seeks carnivorous wholeness, a gluttonous diet of the anatomy of the art–i–verse.

\* \* \*

And while it is rare to attend a poetry festival or a conference and see poets (established and emerging, white and black, academic and non-academic) being treated as equals, consequently it is even rarer to discover literary editors and publishers open to "all" levels of class intelligence. The first task of activism of any perform–a–formist is the removal of all one-dimensional judges of craft.

## Presidential Blackness

[A Race Fearlessness Manifolk Destiny]

We miracles. We have not known true freedom in America or in Art, thus our work has struggled in containers not of our own construction; and yet, within those constraints, we have conjured a magnificent aesthetic toolbox, one that abolitions the flavor locked in foreign forms, one that adds seasoning to secondhand technical devices. Boldly reaching into our own human-handbooks, we are widening—our hybrid, written surfaces exceeding genre and ism. Our vernacular-vision, the way we walk the talk and talk the walk, is its own page-lip-palette of lyric-fixin's. The Independence that once surrounded Nkrumah's head has finally reached us, saturation de conquer root, the motion of destiny!

## One

The first footwork of Race Fearlessness is to
fragment the linearity of the contemporary
literary, color line. A black body, trained-in-the-
tradition, can express a complete thought in as
many movements as it has limbs, broken and
healed. To prevent the community from lining up
behind "A," "The," "I," or predictable proper nouns
and pronouns, both moments of the march
(march-beginning and march-end) must curve
into and from each other like one of Bill Traylor's
"self-taught" snakes of enjambment. Think of
it, this coiling, not as contained in a block or a
stanza, but as the thing that wraps within and
around community, the pictorial schema of black
aesthetic, of lyric progression.

## Two

To make an identity repair kit of all of black folk
behavior, to shine or show off, as nuisance as
nuance, sometimes some-timey and sometimes on-
point, the slanguage of hood ornaments.
Negritude, though often mistaken for primitivism,
has made a comeback as the contemporary
commodity known as swagger. Hear me what I'm
telling you: in addition to offering solidarity to
brothers in prison, blue jeans worn hanging off
the body also mean Kiss my Black ass.

## Three

As it is not possible to "purely" disagree in English, or for African descendants to "truly" agree with England, Race Fearlessness is committed to subject-verb disagreement, its liberating conflict. Yes, there are forms of literacy and illiteracy both capable of innovative revolution, of continuing our collective inner face. A new infinite alphabet pours from the pores of the poor.

## Four

If we close the door and write "Colored Only" on it or "No Whites Allowed," it is not out of a Cult-Nats (Cultural Nationalism) Conceptualism. The only segregation we desire is segregation by choice, a segre-gathering of abundant healing, neither separatism or ghetto-fetish. If we are successful, we will emerge from behind that door capable of forgiving our former owners for cultivating more tokens than true allies of color.

# Five

Our heroic run, back and forth, between "invisibility" and "mask," North and South, and "I" and "We," has strengthened (though fragmented) our consciousness. To bid ourselves a legacy of reference-pride, we are worrying all allusions to Greek mythology (especially Persephone) back into their worn, believed and make-believe exiles, their bad pale labors. It's time for a new passage—one minus the triangular, choir-less trade of great-great-great-grandslaves, one that hangs a signifying sign.

\*　　\*　　\*

Our Negro Heroico is not one of Renaissance or Power or Cutting Edge or Hype or Post Anything. We did not arrive after us, not after Race not after Blackness. Taught long ago to separate "what white folks done to us" from "what we got to do for us," we are no longer hurt in the world, were not hurt into art, and are not above hurting those who continue to take advantage of and hurt the "babymuva" of civilization, Africa. We seek wholeness—not competition, completion—to be rejoined with our many sold-off selves. Equator, belt of civilization, you are our breathing line, the vein of Ra. We seek a Presidential Blackness, ready to break the mouth of yester-morrow, Now.

*Covers-Elect*


I

A red, ringing stimulus.
Well, it could be Michelle calling
but I bet it's Bill.

Handle-yo-business
then bump your fists,
the new religion, a Black-Islamic alliance.
Jeremiah bin Laden.

No Drama Obama ain't no bama,
no veterinarian vetting dogs, no donkey vetoing elephants.
His master's voice, he owns.

All election night
the marble giant sat beneath a lunar vowel,
full moon over Union.
Halo, eclipse, hope.

A portrait to lay the old way of doing things
in Washington to rest,
Presidential Blackness.

## II

They both want the nomination
that's why they both want the phone.
The lobbyist in the lobby is calling.

A profile so Jihad
the flag in the fireplace won't burn
unless you pour
some Halliburton on it.

Cabinet in need of training,
secret files of flea powder. Cabinet on a leash,
Barack's best friends.

Just like the Great Emancipator's mood, the economy
is a financial crisis of stars
in a recession-blue sky
above a credit crunch of columns.

"I, Barack Hussein Obama,
a continental Colored,
do solemnly swear to stay black and die."

# III

Probably just the front desk calling, again,
to complain about
campaign headboard noise.

"You can do this, Boo,"
the Soldierette instructs her tall, hip and athletic,
ivy-league-educated Taliban hubby.
Camouflage à la von Furstenberg.

Revolving-door loyalists
want a partisan, lipstick pit in their ear.
One on all fours.

Consider the marchers
sitting Lincoln has seated with his back to service,
the ghost of battlefields.
Facing freedom freed him.

"The white wig fits
because I have a good wave cap."
George Washington's slaves put his on.

*Godzilla's Avocado*


Tonight, Prophet
is helping Noni make
"creatures," the term

     she "cooked up" for mussels.
     I am "Noni," her
     fake baby daddy,

the one she got
her style from, not her
"soft and buttery"

     bottom lip, that came
     from Mommy. Nonies see things differently.
     Waffles, brown skin.

Lady Liberty making us all healthy
holding up her green
flame of asparagus.

Prophet's a bean eater,
a yummy Kingpin critter.
Run, edamame, run,

the same sun
that rises in orange juice
sets in mac and cheese.

From a lumpy russet, swirling
in a cosmos of miso,
colors mash into casserole.

Kids love kitchens, the sushi chef
re-ending monsters
with embassy-precision.

Life's raw rolls, ready
to unravel the difficult answers
we wrap in seaweed.

"Love is when two people
like the same food
and the same toys,

but war is when lots of people
dress up like salads
and eat each other."

Messy imagination.
All meals need metaphors.
Poems, cutting boards.

An artichoke's heart does not pump ketchup.
It pumps pesto,
oily, olive clots of guacamole.

Prophet is learning
to grow things, including time,
real time, some sense

     of the vitamins of radiance.
     The seedling on
     the window sill, slow to trust sun.

Kids love nature, things smaller than them,
like mushrooms,
cooked into clouds.

     Radiation.
     Fooling time, rushing food,
     hurts the body.

Pesticides are a big deal, poor bees.
The microwave
  hives fear.
Our silver age of dining.

# The Judges of Craft

Thanks for your note. We're actually very interested in poems that address issues of race and racism and wish we could run more of them. Most of what we get in that regard is mere subject matter; that is, there's not enough craft to carry the content (though this is certainly not the case with "Spike Lee at Harvard," which I am sure you'll place somewhere very good).


I

A B C

The act of breathing is the first craft,
the carrier from which
all content pours.


II

The line lives life and life lives the line,
many unbreakable,
broken lifelines.

The human line breaks when it is denied complexity.
The poetic line breaks as a result of complexity.

Tense interruption,
fragment, hiccup,
the rest and rise of inner, linear fracture.
Pre-complete, wholeness.


## III

The goal of breaking
is possibility    nonlinear respiration,
plural not singular.

Breath is community
and community
never competes for residence
or for the approval of the container.

Continuation.
Containment is not permanence.
Confinement is not content.

Culture is home.
The body, its own guest.
Imagination, host.


## IV

Away from identity    way off the shelf of self,
much is read
and must be risked.

The literary chore, rewriting, and being rewritten.

A mask does more
than face judging.
It invites it.    Fits acceptance.

Writing is not king.
Speak.


V

Language prefers inclusion, the income of diversity.

Print did not begin
at the same time as skin. Began because of skin.

Way somewhere in the silence,
in the swelling
progression of chest, the heartfelt hollow.

Where the breathing line c o n t i n u e s,
the breathless line
c a n   n o t.

One fashions a page, a plea, a place for submission.

Style is system.
Culture pours itself into all.
   There is a part of form
that fears pouring.

# VI

In the classroom        the work
on the table is corpse,
surrounded by          other equally

decomposing economies.

Someone in charge decides.
Someone in charge
        designs.

A someone considered worthy of width,
wider than content,
country,
continent.

I have disappointing news, but there's a big silver lining. We discussed your
poems at length and with admiration and excitement, but in the end we
didn't find one in THIS batch that we felt would be a great début for you
in the magazine. It's just that so many of them are about writing, and we try
to shy away from poems explicitly addressing the subject of writing—much
less the politics of the writing scene. But you are definitely on the screen
here, and I'm only (and deeply) sorry I took so long.

# VII

1 2 3

A well-made compromise
allows the shape of exchange into it.
Other currency. Social balance.
The policy of public poetics.

# VIII

The Spoken Page, full of the rage of range,
adds elasticity
to the written word.
        It is the end of waiting.
Mouths must write.

Often craft carries you, off the page, away from control.

Somewhere near the verdict of restraint,
all we do
is compare
one thing to another, servants of "like" and "as."

Often craft prevents you, on the page, from losing control.

The most common gaze
        of portraiture is stare.
        A motionless taste.


# IX

The ribs of an accordion        in contempt
of the geometry of quietude.
All the rules in the handbook
inhaled a long time ago,
the redistribution of respiration.

A dead-end pantoum with dead-end rooms.

Another lengthy case,
a crack in the craft

to crawl through, the trial of proving
      you are flat, worth paper,
mere remembrance.


## X

The body of the book.

Let it flow or let it go      many-wheres
away from being
a deceased thing read into.

There, heard, the seeds of scientific knowledge,
and poems behaving
like novels      the poor reports
of costumed, cloth hearts.

Reading experience
      so bound it paginates the senses.
All five in awe of edition.

Solicit likeness, what they like, the theme is them.


## XI

One of us,
usually a male, tabled,
a contents of none.
      The body, highly rejected.
Net worth, worked,
bio dangling.

They allow you among them
without a hood.
A type of vitiligo typeface
taught taste.

You make the ghetto Greek.
Reference, begging.

Dear Thomas, Lovely to see you the other night. Much as I admire the
stirring aspects of "The Obama Hour" I regret to have to report that its
overall effect is a little too strident for me. Sorry.

XII

All you can say is     What can I say?
Ratio of us to them
far worse than
commas to words.

Reviews of the work somehow a prison, prose.

The patrolled-parole
they feed you.
A straightening tool, control.

There are people to portray and people to betray.

That speech, in print, it drones.
        One tone.
My tongue, a papilla-syllabi.
Anapest good-bye.

## Race Inauguration Day

[A Short Fiction]


Parades, but not-a-one in the meter of a march.
There were parties.
No apology. Then there were more parties.

Still many of our former owners spat at progress,
at celebration, at transparency,
our fought-for step up from nothingness.

Masked, we forgave them.
Civil Wrongs, overcome.

      Statehood!
      No one wants
      to make the hood
            a state.

So we skinned ourselves,
zipper down the body middle,

right there on the National Mall,
the moment the poet,
cold as her tone, enjambed America with "Love."

Without complexion, though,
we looked exactly like
what we had become: a clear people, equal to blur.

Sores.

*A Waste of Yellow*

Up there, the uppity sun.

A thick summer, low luminance, same complexion as honey.

Long light,
the reach of history, its simmering skin of variants,

lightly darkened
or darkly lightened.

Emancipation takes practice.

Such a naturalist you mistranslate heat into hate
every garden.

If nature wants to lighten brown,
let nature lighten brown.

My name is not on any of the cotton I own.

The earth used to be caramel.

## Race Change Operation

When I awake I will be white, the color of law.
I will be new, clean, good; and as pure as snow.
I will remember "being black" the way one
experiences déjà vu, as shadow-memory-feeling.
Race will return to its original association with running
and winning, though I will never have to do either
(ever again) to prove myself Olympic, human or equal.
My English, by fault of gaze (theirs), will upgrade.
I will call my Mama, Mother and my Bruh, Brother
and, as cultural-life-insurance, the gatekeepers will
amputate my verbal nouns and double-descriptives.
When I grow my hair long I will favor Walt Whitman
more than Wole Soyinka. My pale, red neck will scare me,
a frightening irony of freedom. The Literary Party in power
will adopt me, saying "TSE is proof of our commitment
to (verse) diversity. . . ." I am. Narrative poets will use me
as long as they can trust me, and Elliptical women
will want me in their anthologies but not as a colleague.
What will I do with myself other than prove myself,

my whiteness, and that blackness is behind me?
The poetry in my walk will become prose.
I will be a white fiction full of black-ish progression,
the first human bestseller, a Jigga Book Spook.
It will be like having tenure, my value will be done.
This is crazy, this lose-a-world way to whiteness.
What happened to "smiling," to "playing the game,"
to being one of their favorites, to interracial marriage?
As a black, I won a Mrs. Giles Whiting Writer's Award,
so imagine what I will win when I become one of them.
I can see it now, my MacArthur. Jungle eyes, a Guggenheim.
This might be the most racist decision I've ever made
but these lines, unlike the color line, were written to break.
I am tired of lines, of waiting, of lies, my bio full of prizes.
I want my own whiteness, to own then free (someone like) me
even if it means reintegrating another sinking ship.
I'll be that Shine, defiant and drowned, dream alive.

## Sermon on the Unrecognizable
## Shapes of Change

So goes the dream
of evening
the playing field,

but not the pressure of forcing self
into system.

Steal away
to higher education. Take out a loan.
Book.

———————————

Plotless complexion,
my ignorance

was once a complex
and acceptable mode of discipline.
Beneath pigment,

more spectrum,
the inner cosmic level of identity.

———————————

Hood-pride told
my yellow butt to stay put,
no family of.

Homes, big ones,
all left for ghosts.

More than a mortgage
forces movement,
but less than closure is numerical.

———————————

The Streets predate Main.
Many live there.

No curriculum cures pavement.
Certainly not bailout,
corporate Welfare.

The Streets predate Wall.
Many lose there,

———————————

out there, on the stoop, kissing a dog.
No recipient admits this,
this privilege,

although the advantages
are obvious. "Peace,"

the password of gentrification.
We help kill us, displacement,
help them move in.

———————————

All suffer from
the athletic-amnesia

of leasing, our super weakness.
Sunday, too, "team"
is taught. Lord, keep score,

competition is not a gospel.
Renewal, build more.

———————————————

Boring myth needs
a shot of drama,
so we exaggerate everything.

Much like a drum
in a metaphor, or a muffled sermon

on the symptoms of power.
The work wants to last longer
than the life. Life does not.

———————————————

With your work today,
the mechanical way.

Later put a hurtin' on it
to be known, forever, to be felt
when you are away.

With your woman tonight,
the human way.

———————————

The side of the neck,
our favorite radio.
Attitudes need tuning.

I, too, mean to token you.
Talk is strength,

the litter we language with.
Our ranks of defense,
unwritten, unlisted.

———————————

The longer we live
the more "equality" we require.

The United States of Africa America,
a republic of public options.
We age differently.

Population is not continuous,
its balance is unknown.

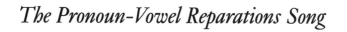

*The Pronoun-Vowel Reparations Song*

mostofthestraighteningisinthetongue

Bongo Jerry

A E I O U,
Y

I O U,

Y

Y–I

Y–O

Y–U

Y

# I BEFORE U

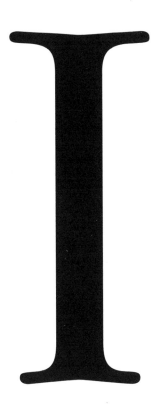

BEFORE U

BEFORE

U

BEFORE

U

I

A   E   U   O   ME

M–E         U–O         ME

AAA—EEE UUU—OOO M—EEEEE

OOOO

U–OOO

U–OOO

M OOOOOO

# E—I
# E—I

O

I

U  D–O–U–B–L–E O,  I

E

I

E

I

OOO  OOO,  I

O A–F–T–E–R U

O

U A–F–T–E–R Q

U

U–O

U–O

U–O

IIIIIIIIIIIIIIIIIIIIIIIIIIIIIIIIIIIII

IIIIIIIIIIIIIIII–E–IIIIIIIIIIIIIII

IIIIIIIIIIIIIII F–I–X IIIIIIIIIIIIII

E     E     E

E     Q

E     U     I

      A

      L     I

I     L     I

      S

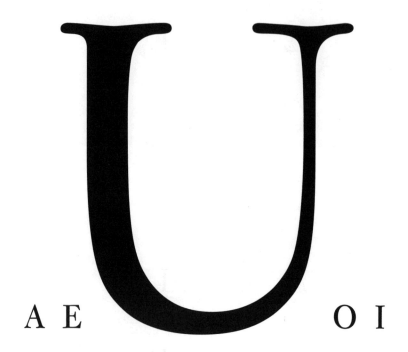

APO
LOG
IZE

## A Few Excuses

It's not my fault
I don't know any.
I can't tell them apart either.

I come from a very traditional family.
Diversity darkens.
It's not my fault.

A Jones drives dad
and a Williams wheels mom.
I can't tell them apart either.

The copyrights of culture.
Blacks acting white. Whites acting black.
It's not my fault.

Class my ass.
He's an elitist. She's too militant.
I can't tell them apart either.

There, "thatone," he seems different.
It's not my fault
he doesn't know many.
Our children won't be able to tell them apart, either.

## Mr. Drum

The music of poetry cannot be external or formal. The only acceptable poetic music comes from a greater distance than sound. To seek to musicalize poetry is the crime against poetic music, which can only be the striking of the mental wave against the rock of the world.

Aimé Césaire

They beat me   To weaken me   Not to imitate breathing  For pleasure not nutrition        In   the   manner   of recreation           In   the   manner of misguided ritual   Out in the open In secrecy     More   of   them   than me   Their kind   Their kin  Their reasoning              Them   forcing themselves on me   Their bodies Their thinking and their feeling  All over me   The global nerve of them

Local hands     Local skills     Local
ideas   In the name of support      In
the name of development      In the
name of dominance    They beat me
Same way they disguise authority
Same way they hide diplomacy     In
their empty empire   Full of markets
Full of forecasts   Full of investments
Invasion and polls and debt    Their
tempo  Their exchanges   Their rates
Property up    Bodies down     All
organized   into worth    Evaluation
and  Performance         Trade and
Promotion    The way they employ
others        Your limbs    their order
The colonial genre      Your useless
usefulness    A nonprofit  That's how
bad they beat me     before I was born
Before I was my own    The beatings
owned me   Owned my rest  My rest
from the rules of labor  Second guess
Show-up late    Protest     All rallies
inside  beaten out   Beneath my skin
Skin I could barely figure out     and
barely  feel while in       Beneath
religion     The  sin  I  was  given
Beneath    intimacy        Beneath
community      Beneath   integrity
Beneath all thefts of me    Their fear
My new arrival  Their feet  Ancestry
and  annotation      My  percussive

human arithmetic Some of The sum
of Their fear Became me Of them
subtracting me A preordered and
divided I Return surrender To
inferior sender I believe I superior
like I was before identity Before I
was dented Before the Atlantic was
formatted Made water commodity
Made humans material Machine
made me Made more like them
Made less me Made here In this
In bed with Agreement In their cold
world image Compromised by
jurisdiction By the limits of their
ways of living Need something
more earthly than meaning Some
thing to fill the puncture in the
ceiling But with a body I belonged
I was volume I was form Shaped
Contained Labeled And with a
label came value The worst
beatings beat me into worth The
decline of the integrity of my own
likeness My oral wouldn't pour
They televised my fall That's how
bad they beat me Till nature refused
me Till nothing came out Till I was
ratings My own Repair Crew Not
just the tube's toolbox My own brew
of unapologetic fixin's Ready to cut
into luxury To option the agenda of

economy   To outlaw profit   I count
To count and be more than counted
the body has to counter crowd
Counter country   If rhythm begins
at the r where meter ends then meter
must end   They beat me   Hacked
me into lines   Into margins   Into
branches   The vernacular owl of
world narrow Wifi   Of wildlife   The
Caucasian sky.

## A Galaxy of Black Writing

[A Universal Course]

American Negro Poetry
Amistad   Betcha Ain't   The Best
of 40 Acres Poetry   Beyond the Blues
Black Arts: An Anthology of Black Creations
Black Creation   Black Dialogue
Black Expressions   Black Fire: An Anthology
of Afro-American Writing   Black Joy
Black Orpheus: A Journal of African
and Afro-American Literature
Black Perspective

Black Poetry: A Supplement
to Anthologies Which Exclude Black Poets
The Black Poets   Black Poets Write On!
Black Review   Black Sister   Black Spirits:
A Festival of New Black Poets
in America   Black Voices: An Anthology
of Afro-American Literature

Black World (Formerly Negro Digest)
Blacktown, U.S.A   The Book of American Negro Poetry
Bopp   The Brass House

The Brown Thrush   Caroling Dusk
Cavalcade   Chant of Saints: A Gathering
of Afro-American Literature, Art,
and Scholarship   Celebrations:
A New Anthology of Black American Poetry
The Children   Confirmation   The Crisis: A Record of the Darker Races
Dices or Black Bones: Black Voices
of the Seventies   Drumvoices:
The Mission of Afro-American Poetry
Early Black American Poets

Ebony and Topaz   Ebony Rhythm   Fire
The Forerunners: Black Poets in America
From the Ashes   From the Belly of the Shark   Freedomways
Giant Talk: An Anthology of Third World Writing
Golden Slippers   Home Girls: A Black Feminist Anthology
Hoodoo   I Am the Darker Brother   It Is the Poem Singing into Your Eyes
The Journal of Black Poetry   Jump Bad
Kaleidoscope: Poems by American Negro Poets
The Liberator   The Magic of Black Poetry
The Messenger   My Black Me: A Beginning Book of Black Poetry

My Name Is Black: An Anthology of Black Poets
Natural Process: An Anthology of New Black Poetry
The Negritude Poets   Negro Anthology   Negro Poets and Their Poems
The Negro Caravan   The New Black Poetry
New Negro Poets: USA   The New Negro Renaissance
Night Comes Softly   Nommo   Obsidian

On Our Way: Poems of Pride and Love
Opportunity: A Journal of Negro Life
The Poetry of Black America   Poetry of Soul:
Poems from Black Africa   Présence Africaine

Primer for White Folks   Roots: A Journal of Critical
and Creative Expression   Shadowed Dreams
Sides of the River   Soon, One Morning
Soulbook   Soulscript   Soulsession
Three Hundred and Sixty Degrees of Blackness Comin'
at You   3000 Years of Black Poetry   Tuesday   We Be Poetin'
We Speak as Liberators: Young Black Poets
Woke Up This Mornin'!   Umbra   Understanding
the New Black Poetry   Yardbird Reader
You Better Believe It

## First Grade, All Over Again

### [1]

When he was little
and just a boy
and called Barry,

his report cards
were shown, first,
to the one person

whose approval
mattered the most,
his mother, Ann Dunham.

Works well with others
who do not work
well with each other.

Another GOP *No*,
another honor roll of polls,
locked-in telephoto.

# [2]

Barry Obama was
African American,
African father, American mother,

but not Barack,
Barack Obama is mixed,
race-less Blackness.

I have seen more photos
of Barack Obama
than I've ever seen

of my own mother.
Blame the Press,
digital photography, all

the camera-phones,
raised like Rockefellers,
above the rest of us.

## [3]

My mother hates
being aimed at. "But Mom, this is
a really good camera,

a Leica." So what, it's
all German to her
and that means torture,

already half locked up
with my brother.
Armed robbery, his war crime.

My parents broke up
the day Jimmy Carter
was inaugurated,

the last time swine
sent to wipe out drug cartels
came home to roost.

## [4]

There's no way to stay
"on-subject" and do this
without high marks

for marksmanship.
Some bald, class bully
taking shots at him,

saying he's not tough.
Saying he's a brown Apologist,
shaking hands with

future allies-of-color
weakens us, so let's waterboard Bo,
the bi-racial Water Dog.

Let's let the human eye decide
if colorblindness is cultural
or regular blindness.

[5]

Mother's Day in the White House,
Marian and Michelle.
First Granny and First Lady.

Out of vernacular-respect,
Black men often refer
to the women they love as "Mama."

This is not something
the minority expects the majority
to accept, reconciliation.

"Once a man loses his mother,
he can accomplish
damn-near anything."

I heard this on the streets
of Washington, D.C.,
right outside the office of citizen.

## *Gone Pop*

[Michael Joseph Jackson]

For Bonnita Joanna Johnson (November 30, 1967–January 15, 2010)

who drove from Cleveland to New York,
said hello and good-bye to her friends,
then drove from New York to Cleveland
    and went to sleep.

The Michael Jackson cacophony is fascinating in that it is not about Jackson at all. I hope he has the good sense to know it and the good fortune to snatch his life out of the jaws of a carnivorous success. He will not swiftly be forgiven for having turned so many tables, for he damn sure grabbed the brass ring, and the man who broke the bank at Monte Carlo has nothing on Michael. All that noise is about America, as the dishonest custodian of black life and wealth; the blacks, especially males, in America; and the burning, buried American guilt; and sex and sexual roles and sexual panic; money, success and despair—to all of which may now be added the bitter need to find a head on which to place the crown of Miss America. Freaks are called freaks and are treated as they are treated—in the main, abominably—because they are human beings who cause to echo, deep within us, our most profound terrors and desires.

James Baldwin

"The Negro…is primarily an artist. … His *métier* is expression rather than action. He is, so to speak, the lady among the races." When the white sociologist Robert E. Park said this in 1918, black intellectuals responded with understandable outrage. Nor did black male musical artists—bluesmen, jazzmen—have any use for this feminized vision of themselves. But Michael has made use of it. He took it up and bound it to a black gay aesthetic that has been pushed to the margins of black culture: drag balls, voguing, club life and biracial and gender bending eros. When Michael and his sister La Toya are photographed side by side, it's as if ghostly twins have just floated out of a gothic mansion. They could be Roderick and Madeline, the tormented siblings in Edgar Allan Poe's "The Fall of the House of Usher." Janet blends right in when the three of them appear together, as they did in court early on in Michael's trial, swathed in flowing white garments, eyes hidden by white-framed dark glasses. The sisters' hair cascaded below their shoulders. Michael's fell softly to his shoulders, then curled upward (the 1960s Jackie Kennedy flip). Their resemblance was uncanny. A war of gender worlds had been going on in the Jackson family for decades, and Michael had a long time ago chosen to join the women.

Margo Jefferson

1

## Falco Berigora

Born Leo, fire, a masculine, extroverted lion.
Born three months and three days before Black Tuesday.
Up from that odyssey, from Fountain Hill
to Oakland to East Chicago to Gary.
An introverted Taurus, full of God's arrows, at his side.
Settled in the steel trap of steel mills, operating cranes.
A brown falcon with green eyes
and falcons like him did not fly, they fathered.
Then fought. Then provided. Then managed.
Favoring, often, the ground, not the sky's traffic of other
talented talons, because the ground favored family.
Poverty's abusive crossroads paved with small prey.
Young sickle-shaped feathers, nine dancing offspring.
Joseph wanted little falcons and got peacocks,
infinite vultures, a lonely prodigy.

2

# Steeltown Boys

Magic City of Steel, The Steel City, U.S. Steel,
All this strength in a regular town with a regular name
    :        Gary,
City in Motion, City of the Century, GI, the G,
county consisting of Lakes, Lake County, Chicagoland,
land of poisonous air, hard to breathe, land hardened by agents,
hardening agents, recording agents like Gordon Keith
        of Steeltown Records.
Gordon was no Gordy, but he was their first big break,
the one who got them "off the ground," off the flat,
t-shaped northwestern corner of Indiana.

A separate class of usefulness for each of their gifts:

> Jackie, tool.
> Toriano, alloy.
> Jermaine, carbon.
> Marlon, nickel.
> Michael, stainless.

Being brothers prevents dislocation. Being brown, corrosion.

School, chores,
rehearsal, talent shows,
travel, strip clubs,
Kingdom Hall.

All the little boy in the studio wants is to be young.
He does not want to be a Big Boy.
He does not want to grow up and get the girls
like his brothers. All he wants is bubblegum.
All this rust-resistance in a regular family with a regular name
      :     Jackson.
Motto: We are doing great things.

3

# Three Screws

[Prince, Prince, Jr., Prince III]


Gone now, but (in life) each executed a proper turn.
Each progressed family,
the dominant leg of social order.
The first Prince was a slave,
assigned, after passing, the well-being of his great granddaughter,
    Katherine Screws,
but even an ancestor, the best carrier of care,
couldn't protect her
from polio, the husband of her childhood.
There are parts of marriages that are wars,
    and parts of wars
that are marriages, nasty civil ones.
Prince becomes a tenant farmer. Prince, Jr., a farm owner.
    When Joseph is unfaithful,
the ghost of Prince punishes him with extra work,
the heavy cotton of potato picking.

To rescue his mother from all of the farmers
    and the failed musician,
little Michael dreams he is a prince, harsh on his peasant brothers,
    but nice to rodents
like mice and his bone-crushing snake.

(La Toya, the anti-Tito, a revenge-masterpiece.)

    Katherine's father,
    Prince Albert Screws,
    Prince III,
    Michael's grandfather

migrates from Barbour County, Alabama,
the birthplace of a ghoulish man with a paralyzed face,
the King of Southern Populism.

Ghosts, even kindred ones, don't work for free.
They expect benefits, left and right,
and input—lifelong levels of fright constant as the thin
    royalties of sibling rivalry.
There are things, scary things, no one can protect a child from,
like a broken guitar string,
but apparitions, like the ones haunting Katie's walk,
have been here before for a reason.
The older brothers are maturing, their dreams
more male than Michael's and Marlon's, and every flicker in
Suzanne de Passe, their gorgeous

    Cherokee, French,
    Bahamian, Russian,
    and Caribbean coach.

is a phantom supreme.

Water balloons are falling, boyhood about to burst.
Which doors to be afraid of
and which doors to frighten from?
For this reason Suzanne nicknamed
        Michael, Casper.

# 4

## "Lemme Tell You Now"

Detroit is not Gary. Gary is in Indiana.
Detroit, Michigan. It is not the G. It is the D.
The D has a reputation for being dangerous and invincible.
The D does not make steel; it is made of steel.
If the D and the G were people,
they might be attracted to each other.
Michigan is famous for automobiles.
Indiana (or Indy) for speed.
Part "Goin' Places," part "Moving Violation."
If signed, the family will have to move,
first Joe and the boys,
then Katherine, the girls
and the baby boy:

     Rebbie,
     La Toya,
     Janet
     and Randy.

The material they used in the G
would not work in the D, so the group had to bend.
Motown made stars like Ford made cars.
Charm school.
Weekly, quality control meetings.
Family, a corporation.
The Corporation, a hit factory
with a blue, stenciled M on it.
The audition tape is famous, so let's skip it.
"Sign them," not their Steeltown skin.
Gordy doesn't want anything to do with Black Power
unless it's cute. Think "Dancing in the Streets,"
not "(Sittin' on) The Dock of the Bay."
Detroit is not Memphis. Memphis is in Tennessee.
Detroit, Michigan. It is not Soulsville.
It is Hitsville. Hitsville will lose another engine
        if Motown leaves Michigan.
Motor town, a portmanteau,
families and friends forced into crowded rearview mirrors.
Ed Sullivan was lied to, too.
A Diana did not discover them. A Gladys did.
"I may be young but I know what it's all about."
Michael was eleven years old, not nine, the two years they took away
        not enough
to give back what he'd already lost.

5

## The Black Beatles

The screaming girls at the airport
want brothers. They want to race, not run,
their fingers through Afros
the shape of gold records.
The kinky work of pleasure as natural
as the kinky work of struggle.
The only mop tops they've known drag wet floors.
Want to be wanted back and schooled,
"i before e except after c."
"Maybe Tomorrow" not "Yesterday,"
        longing not loss.
Their invasion, a soul-sation, comes from within.
It is not from England; it is not British.
Favorite sport, Jackson-chasing,
ages and heights to match their own ages and heights.

The only thing more exhaustive
        than 1970 was 1971,
the large hysterical crowds.

Four consecutive number one hits:

        "I Want You Back," Libra,
        "ABC," Pisces,
        "The Love You Save," Taurus,
        "I'll Be There," Virgo,

but four is not enough of a crush. Five is.
Four is fab, Fab Four. Five, one more.
A chance for "ABC" to kiss "Let It Be," for
"The Love You Save" to stalk "The Long and Winding Road."
Hard to hear anything, in concert, because
of the screaming fan club positioned at the top of the charts,
the number of weak knees at number one.

Teen hearts everywhere. Hearts on posters,
heart stickers, sewable heart patches.
Jackson Five coloring books.
A J5 45 on the back of a cereal box. Cut it out.

        Tito heart Dee Dee,
        Jermaine heart Hazel
        and everyone hearts Michael.

Cartoon portraits, framed by hearts.
Color draining Blue Meanies, hustling a yellow submarine
        out the back door.
Heart-shaped stars on their dressing-room doors.
Johnny's heart, two tragic drums, stabbed in the snare.

Soul merchandising, groovy valentines,
     the bass line's, heart-burst finish of darling throbs.
A heart at the bottom of a cursive *J*.
A heart at the bottom of a cursive *S*.

    *Right On!*

# 6

## Automatic Systematic

Like an illusion the cuteness either wore off
     or was worked off,
or both, out there in the constant sunshine, chests out
in bare-chested, West Hitsville
where, out there, the material (they were
given) gradually weakened.
Think "Rockin' Robin," boys imitating birds.
Think "Ben," a ballad to a rat.
This would not have happened in the D.
Fail to chart (in the D)
and you were taken apart, right there
where it mattered, in Studio A, the snake pit of hits.
Fail again and you were never reassembled
     or scrapped for parts,
saying what you said you never can say, "Good-bye."
The sun changed their bodies,

their bodies changed their voices.
Never a clear calendar, always something on it,
        if not acne, then
sessions, studio-produced like seasons.
If not motorbikes, starting and stopping,
        then the motors of Disco,
stopping and starting, like an earthquake locked in Campbellock.
A smart mime will either dance differently
        or dry up,
not one but all five, bodies down to the ground.
Nature, fractured to a fault, has to be somewhat responsible
for mankind's mechanical behavior.

 

    The sun    the sets
    the dime    the stops
    the ro       the bots.

# 7

## Bye Bye 5

You could feel it.
It was special,
another dimension.

It was natural
and untouchable, a congruent mark of birth.
   It was 5
and it did not belong to them.

It belonged to him.
He who trademarked it.
He who signed them.

Refer to him as "he" and as "some people"
like we don't know him
   because most Sagittarians
like the upper hand.

If they take the 5 with them,
    they might hurt it.
If they don't take the 5 with them,
    it might hurt them.

A Jackson-Gordy wedding.
A marriage tougher than any audition.
Katherine's 2 divorce petitions,
    2 rescinded.

Some people just can't
    control their feet,
former Golden Gloves sparring over
    artistic control.

*J* tired of 5, 5 tired of *J*.
    Now Jermaine is a second son
in two demanding families.
Sometimes it takes a legal battle
    to be loved.

8

## Brotherly *Triumph*, *Destiny* Love

Good times, enjoying themselves, posterized.

Let them show you
living together, the lipstick of it.
Grown-up, blowout kits smiles, the result of recording freedom.
Michael's clapping begins the celebration.
Marlon's necklace, Marlon's vest, his style of life
      makes the cover pop.
Tito, think happy, Tito, this is the least like Joseph
      you've looked in years.
Green for the eldest. Natural Jackie. Arm around Randy.
Being younger than Michael is the only way to replace Michael
without really replacing Michael.
Randy's first time on an LP cover with his brothers.
First time Jermaine was not, but *that's how loss goes.*
Motown didn't leave them; they left Motown.

A new contract, two new labels, a union of logos:
Epic's open, scripted italics.
Philly International's symbol for balanced love, Ps of intercourse,
      one up and one down.
The only thing solo, in the photo, is Michael's thoughts.
He can feel "Can You Feel It" already,
the weight of fashioning all forthcoming voyages,
if not every song, on his shoulders.
The strength of one man, his pre-superstar skin
      unbuttoned to a victory.
All ten eyes in step as their brotherly noses.
They are young men now. They've learned how to work
female-shaped, soft, male mouths.

9

## A Scare A Crow A Pea A Cock

Every morning, for five hours, mirrors are polite again.
The man in it, the one resembling a hidden him
and the one hiding him accepts this:

   the fright wig,
   the coil legs
   and the tomato nose.

All made up, all of a slow-sudden, to scare nothing
but his blues away. His blues are pimples.
His pimples are witnesses, everywhere, ready to eat in front of him
      and ready to eat off of him.
He's a vegetable, and veggies have enemies.
Abusive birds think of him as tenement entertainment.
Most can read scare but scare can't read them,
not without the straw stuff of

Bacon,
Confucius,
Socrates,
Cicero,

the scraps of wisdom he counters emptiness with.
Crows remind him, "without a brain,
     you can't get down."
Knock-kneed walk. Bigfoot spin.
The real Wiz is Q, Q for his saturated emerald scores.
Q for his bar-b-que love, of.
Not all peacocks are brilliant. Not all crows are dull.
The boys had seen their first train of eyes
     at Gordy's mansion,
the day Michael first wished he was Berry's son,
but Jermaine beat him to it, legally,
so he beat Jermaine to everything else, naturally.
Family-hurt, fully fanned and iridescent, hotels the heart.
La Toya screamed for them because,
     being Joe's boys,
they could not scream for themselves.
Slow piano, cello coda.
Embroidered robes, all edged in glow.
Brown peafowls, a unit of sound of them, time kept with
     pointing necks,
their signature, adult choreography of blame.

# 10

## Sonic Personality

Alone in the magic.
Thunder thumbs to heart, mummified heart. Heart to hand,
    glittering hand.
Hand to crotch, a c c u s e d crotch.
More kick and stuff.

    Pose, fedora on.
    Drama-pelvis.
    Kick and leave leg up to tap it.
    Arm-jitsu, turn.
    Kick and leave leg up to tap it.
    Quick cat in a cat stance,
        vogue-crisp.
    Fedora off, pose
    and stare at it a grand second, tossed fabulous.
    Clap. Open triangle,

big masculine hands around the defendant.
Click. Pretend to comb.
Click, click.
Switch sides to comb.
     Flow.
Pocket imaginary comb.

Mic grab, slap. Mic grab, choke. Smelly's mad at it for not being ON.
Smelly's trying to hide the size of it with his hands
but Big Nose ain't having it.
Smelly counters with a new look: a Jheri curl, rhinestones
     and surgery, plastic.
First a favor, the old songs,
"I love those songs, those were magic moments
with all my brothers, including Jermaine."
Run from or rush through the medley of family just once more.
". . . Those were good songs.
I like those songs a lot, but especially I like—"

Alone in the jelly.
Lyricon denial to reverb, defiant reverb. Reverb to hiccup,
     womanized hiccup.
Hiccup to crotch, a n g r y crotch.
A gnawing bass.

    Unhuhuhnuhuh *hee* (point). Unhuhuhnuhuh *woo* (point).
    Mime a throw, look both ways, spin.
    Pull pulled-up pants up,
    show-off socks, sock-tease.
    Again-a-look again-both-ways,
       famous pause.
    Show the microphone.

Ready to glide backwards
K L A W N O O M, drag ball to heel.
Gravity's *avi* replaced by feet,
three seconds of air,
lunar spin, toe-stop.

A real photograph, a real letter and a real gun
not a visual trick like wearing white socks to highlight
        your feet, but real mental illness
like baby hair, frozen in a webbed slide, on the sides
        of a grown man's face.
Baby oil, not grease, is the word.
Mixing a nervous breakdown ninety-one times can't hide
        your real snake, not Muscles,
the one that eats more than interviewers.
Yet, such royalty deserves extra royalties.
Astaire, an admirer.
Dates with Brooke, dates with Tatum.
Liza, a weird friend. Liz, a weirder white mother.
A public appearance and an intimate photo
with a black woman other than Diana Ross
        might help.
The moment you do, in a video, you turn into your middle name.
        You get Joseph's eyes.
". . . be careful what you do," jump-kick with a twist.

The shaking hand gestures No, kick.
Right leg possessed,
        fist, fist in glove,
twist, open fist.
A fury that sparkles.
A fury that stands the mic, grabs.

A mercy, weakening.
Body lowers, body rises.
Spin-a-versary to the edge, insistence.
Ankle action, four forward moments
       in search of reverse.
Lastly, a bow, classic,
point down point up,
but first, stomp the ground.


Alone in Katherine's jacket.
Door-to-door to paradise, the kingdom's paradise. Paradise
       to truth, awake the truth.
Truth to the witness, Jehovah's Witness.
Applause, a Paris, burning.

## 11

## Ola Ray

There are many ways to read *Thriller,* the video.

My favorite is that it's a metaphor
for Joe and Katie's courtship.
Them on a date, in a film within a film, then a real life warning,
    "I'm not like other guys."
O beautiful trusting Katie, O sly monstrous Joe.
When the moon says "Werewolf," a man must Werewolf.
The rest is sex hate. Michael was scared of *it*
(he had his reasons), so he frightened her
and pranked her and taunted her, in rehearsals, with "Brooke,
    Brooke is coming!"
Fool, Ola Ray was so fine she was a lie,
a good one, like Technicolor.
A black pin-up with a runway vibe and a matinee smile,
nearly Dandridge.

34 (Bust)
23 (Waist)
35 (Hips)

Verse        Beauty        Story
Some modeling in St. Louis . . . in a band in Japan.
Landis liked her work in *Playboy*, the nudity, the freedom.
Michael loved her walk, wanted to borrow it,
     and did,
but her fake-fright put him right back
under his brother's hotel beds, hiding and spying,
while they had sex with fans. Her b u t t was his,
and she was willing, but, again, Michael was scared of *it*.
He only wanted to pretend-monster,
never a real zombie or wolfman like the producers
who expected sexual favors from her:

     *Body and Soul* (1981)
     *Night Shift* (1982)
     *48 Hrs.* (1982)
     *The Man Who Loved Women* (1983)
     *10 to Midnight* (1983)
     *Beverly Hills Cop 2* (1987)

That's what you get, bad bit parts, for being pretty.
Get sent to Germany to pick up a Grammy you get to keep.
Owed so much more, so no one blames you,
     all those brothas watching MTV
just to see you—a hot black, music video, damsel-in-distress.
Robin Givens and Nola Darling
     rolled into one
two-piece, light blue, leopard strut, cream-scream,
our horro-tica noir thrill.

# 12

# Typhoon Michael

He's too much to be a person. He just a people.

James Brown

One of Japan's seasonal storms, Mai-ke-ru,
	has caused another vigil.
Boys and girls, young right hands, offered to gloves,
leather pants, and black and metal studs.
An Asian Negro, a yellow one, writes the word "Bad" in blood,
	graffiti blood,
on the paper wings at Narita International Airport.
Begins a trend: bleached skin, mascara, the cleft chin
	and the butch, bitch-strutting
into press conferences with Bubbles, a chimp.
Empire of the bandaged arm, hair tied back, the late crotch-dynasty.
Michael is his own action figure,
the ambassador of military rhythm and Tokyo loves it.
In Osaka, the key to the city,

to murder, to magic, to the minutia of motion
     of bodies folding,
     of marching,
one massive origami zilla.
Hospital visits, orphanages. Donations to charities.
Tickets hanging, like cranes,
left for underprivileged children.
Years in a family-group designed like a bento box
     and now this, his first solo tour,
a world tour, nominated for tour of the year:

     16 months,
     123 concerts,
     4.4 million fans,
     15 countries,
     $125 million gross,

a soft drink's soft money, all proceeds payable to PepsiCo.
Tour sponsor, two commercials, one inferno.
Not a thing to throne, pyrotechnics.
Not a thing to be king of, a generation.
Every taste test, a yes, some guy in some other group
     would have done more than blink
for a share of the market shares.
Coke did not wish it were Pepsi any more than Pepsi
     wished it had taken more precaution.
The angrier the dancer, the more at-risk the dance attacker.
A kiss can be like striking a match, forbidden.
Tatiana hired and Tatiana fired, both times for fires.
Captain, eventually, of his own burn center
     of failed three-dimensional dawns,
but not of this fiery world.
The planet must make the planet make that change.

# 13

## Wacko Jacko

He's a very sweet, down-to-earth person. A lot like me.

Naomi Campbell

The tabloids can't keep up with the surgeries,
the collecting, the animals, the shopping, all the candy wrappers
left like tabs everywhere,
so they make things up, things
hideous as hearsay, weird things, we believe:

He and Janet
are the same person.
Diana Ross is his lover.
They got married,
and adopted Webster.

The bandaged, leftover nose—a rhino.
Lips, a tattoo, not a relief but a permanent painting of a kiss.

Predators, like female owls, in both eyes.
Mouth, a sharp snake. Snake, a pale cave.
The wildlife in the songs comes from
the same venom stubble comes from, testosterone, the body's land
     of seized porn.
Boy actors, special friends, alcohol to minors.

       The Elephant Man's bones,
       how much would something
       like that cost?

All he needs is rest, not the kind that immediately morphs
into a photo of him in an oxygen chamber,
     not his nightly media-funeral of insomnia.
Fame loves fame, but fame that hates fame spreads fame-hate.
Paparazzi like commas.
The tip of the nose is real, the tip of the nose is a prosthetic
but he can afford it: the expensive peace,
of speechless, bleached skin.
The only things entertaining has left for him to rule
     are all carnival and zoo-like,
but every fairy tale needs the daughter of a king
if it ever wants to become a Pop Empire, someone to say Never
(since his handlers won't) and someone to add grace,

     a little Priscilla,
     a princess,
     a Presley.

What to do with her after the make-up of damage control
     never wore off?
The record of their break-up, already broken

long before the awkward, televised kiss.
You know what they say about men with large, blotched hands
    and big blotched feet.
The only d she got was divorce.
Only certain types of touching allowed, a heaven they faked.
    You saw the video: skin glowing like a vow,
vow glowing like a lie, love's lie, a smooth cry.

      "I love you."
      "I love you more.
      Blanket me."

# 14

## White Skin, Black Surgical Masks

"We are...,"
but what "we"
  are we

if a body,
  gifted too
many gods,

  black vs.
white, male
  vs. female,

locks itself
  in infinite
surgery,

wellness
vs. wealth, the
  operating

tables of Pop.
  Pharmacies, nearby,
remastered.

  Panic attacks
dance floor blood
  every track.

For recovery, Slash.
  For vitiligo,
make-up,

  translucence,
the cellophane glow
  of pigment

incognegro,
  dermatology
vs. nutrition.

  If race a
transvestite, penis
  a dalmatian

prescribed protection,
  the tight
green latex of

bedtime fantasy,
". . . straight on
      till . . ." the

nomadic, black
    fashions
of "morning."

   Children
don't heal when
    hidden in

the damaged
    lungs of mileage.
Bahrain

    to Ireland,
Ireland to the Platinum
    Triangle.

Paradise sequins,
    saturates,
platelet and palette,

    but all brown
boys, except one,
    stay black.

The rest,
    left alone,
"can wait."

## 15

## The Last Anti-Gravity Lean Dream

June tried to choke Google but the truth,
gaudy and eccentric as the magnetic sun, defended itself,
out running the Internet like one last supernova rumor.
This is it. This is pull. This is what happens,
equally and often, when the earth and the sky continue to call.
The body, stuck in the middle, considers living.
The body, stuck in the middle, considers dying.
Spirit needs seclusion. Mind, illusion,
another spotless Kingdom; the playful, false drugs of Disney.
This can't be the end, but most of the unhealed world
has already half-heard it, either,
the old fashion way, on car radios or from CNN.
But no one heard it the way family
      will always hear it.
Tito, by phone from Janet, on the freeway crying.
To the Jack5ons, the helicopters over Los Angeles are sad angels

above a cathedral of mayhem.
A mother and a father has lost one of its grown babies,
the most famous of their famous children,
the most talented of the talented brothers.

     Yes, Maya, "We Had Him," he was ours,
all of him—the needle marks, clusters of bruises, and burnt scalp.
Although the lighter his skin got
the more unlike us he got. Still, privately,
we defended him, everything except the sleepovers
and the pajamas, settled in court and out.
Tragic mulatto, triumphant albino.
Faith loves to undo privacy.
Privacy loves to court addiction, addicted to repetition.
Rehearsals, the same routines
over and over, sharp as incisions,
not one but two autopsies.

        Valium,
        an anxiety drug,
        a sedative.
        Valium,
        an anxiety drug,
        a sedative.

Only one thing has ever felt like performing,
being put under, the sexual worriless rest of anti-gravity-lean
      love,
a world rocked, Mercury on tiptoes, butterflies.

## Absolute Otherwhere

[Cave Canem  2009]

We know there's a recognizable We,
  an I-identifiable many.
That right there that's me,
  one of the us from us who see us.

Retreat to attack, an Otherwhere of others
  who are other than Other.
Equality will skin you
  if you don't exceed ISBN.

Been told before, before you forgot,
  before you hadn't been to.
Barely matters where, after you didn't get back,
  back to, before being left out.

There are small Black settlements
  throughout every alphabet.
After work, whipped, for smothering
  the canon with cocoa butter.

Got a gift for you, us-sales aside,
    there's more to words than becoming books.
A challenge for you, You-ness.
    Add yours.

# Roots

The author wishes to thank the editors and readers of the following publications, programs and websites where these poems originally appeared, often in slightly different form—

*The American Poetry Review:* "The Judges of Craft"
*The Baffler:* "Race Inauguration Day"
*Bat City Review:* "Song On"
*Black Renaissance Noir:* "A Galaxy of Black Writing," "Audience,"
    "The Identity Repair Man," "Race Change Operation"
*Callaloo:* "A Waste of Yellow," "AWS Ode," "Covers-Elect,"
    "The Pronoun-Vowel Reparations Song"
*Columbia: A Journal of Literature and Art:* "Mr. Drum"
*Jubilat:* "Skin, Inc."
*The Kenyon Review:* "Understanding the New Genuine Negro Hero"
*Lit:* "The Return of *Colored Only*"
*The Nation:* "Mr. Dynamite Splits"
*The Oxford American:* "Presidential Blackness"
*Pluck!:* "My Meter Is Percussive"
*Poetry:* "Or," "The New Perform-A-Form"
*Rattle:* "A Few Excuses"

*Reverie:* "Absolute Otherwhere"

*www.theRoot.com:* "The Obama Hour"

*The Splendid Table* (NPR): "Godzilla's Avocado"

*Starting Today: 100 Poems for Obama's First 100 Days:* "First Grade, All Over Again"

*Tin House:* "Smudge," "Ways to Be Black in a Poem"

*Zoland Poetry:* "No Easy Task," "Spike Lee at Harvard"

"A Galaxy of Black Writing," "As Segregation, As Us," "No Easy Task," "The Return of *Colored Only*" and "Ways to Be Black in a Poem" appeared in the chaplet *Song On* (WinteRed Press 2005).

"AWS Ode" is dedicated to Chinua Achebe and was read to him at a luncheon for the dedication of The Achebe Center, Bard College, May 18, 2009.

"Covers-Elect" signifies on "I'll Get It!," "The First," "The Politics of Fear," "Reflection," and "Vetting," Presidential campaign covers created by Barry Blitt, Drew Friedman, and Bob Staake for the *New Yorker.*

"Godzilla's Avocado" is dedicated to Kellie Knight and Prophet Lee Davison and was commissioned by the Poetry Foundation and recorded for *The Splendid Table* (NPR, Washington, D.C.) on June 2, 2009.

"Mr. Dynamite Splits" was reprinted in *Spoken Word Revolution Redux,* and the photographs that accompany it were taken by the author at the memorial service for James Brown held at the Apollo Theater. A few of the photographs originally appeared in *Indiana Review.*

"Mr. Drum" is dedicated to Henry Nxumalo, *Drum* magazine's most courageous investigative journalist. Henry fought to expose injustice, cruelty, and narrow-mindedness and was murdered in 1957 while investigating a piece.

"The New Perform-A-Form" was performed at "Futurism and the New Manifesto: Celebrating 100 Years of the Founding and Manifesto of Futurism," Museum of Modern Art, New York City, February 20, 2009.

"Presidential Blackness" was reprinted in *The Best American Poetry 2010* (Scribner), edited by Amy Gerstler, series editor: David Lehman.

"Race Change Operation" was written for the exhibition "Afrofuturism" and read at Spaces Gallery (Cleveland, Ohio), June 3, 2006.

"Race Inauguration Day" was reprinted in the *Alhambra Poetry Calendar 2010 Anthology*, selected by Shafiq Naz.

"Smudge" was commissioned by *"Writers* on View" and written in response to "Abstraction, Figuration, and the Spiritual. David Stern: The American Years 1995–2008," and read at the Yeshiva University Museum (New York City), January 28, 2009.

"Understanding the New Genuine Negro Hero" was reprinted in the 2011 *Pushcart Prize XXXV: Best of the Small Presses*, edited by Bill Henderson with the Pushcart Prize editors.

"Ways to Be Black in a Poem" was reprinted in *Under the Rock Umbrella: Contemporary American Poets from 1951 to 1977*, and as a broadside at the Poetry Center of Chicago.

Many thanks to the Akwaaba Literary Mansion (Washington, D.C.), the Atlantic Center for the Arts, Blue Flower Arts, Bread Loaf Writers' Conference, Cave Canem, Efuru Guest House (Harlem), *Mosaic* Magazine, the Wave Poetry Bus, Mrs. Giles Whiting Writers Foundation, and the numerous photographers and poets who looked at photos and commented on the poems. The cover photograph of Chinyere Evelyn Uku was taken at Kramerbooks & Afterwords Cafe in Washington, D.C., in 2009, and the majority of "Gone Pop" was written at Common Grounds: A Neighborhood Coffee House, 376 Tompkins Avenue, Brooklyn, New York.

# About the Author

Thomas Sayers Ellis was born and raised in Washington, D.C., and attended Paul Laurence Dunbar High School. He is a photographer and a poet and co-founded The Dark Room Collective in Cambridge, Massachusetts, in 1988 before receiving an MFA from Brown University in 1995. He is the author of a chapbook, *The Genuine Negro Hero* (Kent State University Press, 2001), a chaplet, *Song On* (WinteRed Press, 2005), and his first full collection *The Maverick Room* (Graywolf Press, 2005) was awarded the John C. Zacharis First Book Award. His poems have appeared in numerous journals and anthologies. He is the recipient of a Whiting Writers Award and has been awarded residencies at the MacDowell Colony, the Fine Arts Work Center, and Yaddo. He teaches at Sarah Lawrence College and in the low-residency creative writing program at Lesley University, and he is on the faculty of Cave Canem. He lives in Brooklyn, New York, and in Washington, D.C., in the summer.

Book composition by BookMobile Design and Publishing Services, Minneapolis, Minnesota. Manufactured by Maple Vail on acid-free paper.